Internet marketing – A New Approach

Internet marketing – A New Approach

Ray Griffin

Published in the United Kingdom by Weblake Ltd

www.plannedsites.com

ISBN-13: 978-1497521353

Printed in the United States of America

Book and Jacket Design: www.pencilpusherdesign.com

First Edition

DEDICATION

To all cats everywhere especially Jeeves, Bobby, Thelma,

Louise and Roni

CONTENTS

ACKNOWLEDGMENTS

This project (book and accompanying website) was floundering until GailSuperStar arrived. After struggling for a year or two trying to transform my prose into something readable I gave up and started to look on the internet for someone with style who could take my scribblings and present them professionally.

GailSuperStar came from two directions. The first was as one of a batch who could write English. I initially chose to pursue her for the totally illogical reason that she lives only a few miles from me. She then came up on her own website as something else altogether – a graphic designer with website tendencies. No mention of copywriting. I was intrigued and pursued her to her phone number. I couldn't believe I'd found a copywriter whose main work was in graphic design and websites. But I had. She did a couple of jobs for me, proved outstanding in all areas (run-of-the-mill average doesn't earn you Super Star billing) and my book and website were transformed from a pathetic work-in-progress in remarkably short time.

Ancestry.co.uk (us websites must stick together) would have you believe that GailSuperStar is formally known as Gail Watson. She is a remarkable, old-fashioned polymath. Fluent in English and Scouse, she has a first-class degree from Liverpool University in English Language and an HND in graphic design. She has qualified in the University of Life in photography, website architecture, HTML, CSS and the 80/20 power-curve.

Gail is a freelancer and you'll find more information on a special page of her site, a page built for readers of this book, pencilpusherdesign.com/PlannedSites. But be warned: such talents in one person are valuable commodities.

Jackie Rickman is a daughter to be proud of but that's not why she features here. She's here because she's of a different generation (in other words the people I'm writing for), street-wise, literate and numerate. She has a family to look after including a six-month old daughter, a full-time job and a house to keep. Into all this she gladly slotted critical appraisals of important chapters and her contributions laid waste a veritable undergrowth of rubbish so we could all see the wood for the trees.

Jay Burke is Jackie's partner. He is Gold Certified by Microsoft in something very geeky but, whatever it is, he works as the Chief IT Infrastructure Engineer for

Liverpool's best known wealth management and broking firm. Being Jackie's partner he was a sitting duck when I was looking for a further opinion on various parts of the book. His incisive comments were startling to the extent they led to some in-depth re-thinking on aspects we blithely took as read; they showed the value of coming to a subject from an unusual angle.

INTRODUCTION

The newness of these media is what can often both attract and trip up new users. Many of the techniques of internet marketing are not only new there are often no parallels in traditional marketing and attempts to mix them can be fatal. Google AdWords, for instance, is not a substitute for traditional advertising; it is a unique approach to attracting customers that has to be implemented with complementary, equally innovative, procedures.

Many techniques used to increase online profits have been and are still being developed, constantly improving previous results.

We now know there is a minimum requirement, a spread of tools and techniques that can be harnessed and used to achieve lift-off – without the risk of losing money, time and effort in the process.

What is internet marketing?

It does exactly what it says on the tin. Marketing products

online, usually initiated by a buyer (consumer or business) using a computer (including tablets and mobile phones) and a payment card to buy goods or services.

The whole transaction from start (search by user) to finish (delivery of product to door) can be carried out online. Digital products can be delivered even faster - straight to desktop or tablet in a matter of seconds. Amazon does not call it 'One Click' buying for nothing.

In internet marketing, then, the buyer is making things easy for herself by using many technical innovations to replace the time and effort in going out, searching the High Street (or many High Streets) buying what she wants (hopefully) and then bringing it home.

The seller, though, is in a completely new world. He has to invest in a website designed to handle what he quickly learns is called eCommerce, find the means to bring qualified prospects to his website and to create a feeling of trust in the website for the buyer to make a purchase. He then has to get the customer to repeat the process regularly so he can elevate him to the status of 'regular customer'

Fringe phenomena

Many changes in related activities have been seen in the wake of the increased use of internet marketing. The rise and rise in the number of courier companies whose vans are everywhere has become familiar. This has led to real competition in the levels of service. Ten years ago we were expected to stay in all day on the expected day of delivery. Now we are warned of impending delivery by email and sent a text message telling us the actual delivery time to the nearest hour.

While we're on the subject consider delivery policies

themselves: fierce competition between companies are seeing offers such as:

- Free-of-charge deliveries
- Many sites now willing to take returns AND pay return delivery.
- Choice of days and times of delivery
- Alternative shipping addresses
- Online tracking of purchases

In my view these were inevitable because accountants would realise cost allocations needed closer examination. Profits on online sales shouldn't be contributing to retail overheads but could be used to help make online offers more attractive.

One of the features of the dot com boom (remember that, at the very end of the last millennium?) was investors ploughing huge amounts of money into companies set up just to exploit this new way of ~~making~~ losing money – that was ill-thought out and massively hyped.

They didn't even bother with a telephone number (how quaint). Website promoters thought telephones were out-dated and phones were going to become extinct. Nowadays the savvy marketer has her phone number prominently displayed at the top right of every page of the site. The really adept operator shows a genuine BT land-line number (not the discredited 08xx numbers that Oftel should have sorted out long ago) that are answered by human beings straight away. See Chapter 13 for more trenchant comments on this subject.

It used to be said that a website had eight seconds to persuade a visitor to stay rather than click on the Back button. Now research shows that figure is actually nearer two seconds.

Amazon

Amazon is a star to follow. It is a rare survivor of the dot-com boom and bust and even rarer for being so successful that many internet marketers follow its every move and update. The layout of their pages is not accidental; it has evolved over many years and tested at all stages for the optimum sales results and growth. The way they treat their customers is exemplary including their 'One Click' buying facility, an internet first and widely imitated.

The Amazon phenomenon has become a juggernaut and it will be interesting to see down what road it leads us. Starting as a book store it is now a department store that seems limited (at the moment) only by its inability to supply fresh food.

Smaller websites and companies are often intimidated by the breadth and ambition of Amazon. It is often said that our strengths can often become our weaknesses (and vice versa). With Amazon, its ubiquitous nature and size can often dominate a market, but leave gaps for companies willing to compete in areas such as specialist sectors and unique items that cannot be purchased at big box retailers. Don't forget we all start equal on a Google search results' page.

SEO

SEO is so well known and so often written about that we hardly need explain it stands for Search Engine Optimisation.

It will come as a surprise to most people that SEO is in great transformation – and a lot of the old obsession with building (artificial) links, keyword stuffing, comment posting and mendaciousness in all its forms is dying a death. And we have to be grateful for that. It means a more even playing field for everyone, and the freedom to create great and useful content that will get found.

We can be confident of that as the chief slayer of bad SEO practice is Google itself. Google can't stand artificial SEO and this is what makes its demise certain.

Google does more to protect web searchers than it does for any other class of stakeholders. Its users are more important to Google than advertisers (who give it 97% of its $59bn income) or its shareholders or its employees. Searchers, says Google, are the life-blood of the company.

Google takes the view that whichever way you look at it SEO is just a series of tricks that attempt synthetically to manipulate search page rankings and that is not in the best interest of searchers to allow it. Just produce, Google says, a properly structured website with original, relevant, attractive content. You should include your keywords in your titles and headers (depending on what website or development platform you use, they will be referred to as 'Title' or 'Header') and content. If you do this, Google continues, the pages and search rankings will take care of themselves.

A couple of years ago we were asked to advise on a sports' equipment supplier's website whose pages were ranked somewhere round the bottom of page one/top of page two. Not bad but they wanted to do better and their webmaster had started completing what he thought was SEO to improve the situation and the site sank without trace. (Not quite, actually, as we used some tracing software and found it on page 52.) To start with we looked at the cricket equipment page. The word 'cricket' appeared 164 times on that page, twenty-odd times in the main content (bad enough) but the rest 'hidden' in the page footer. (Text can be hidden by formatting it in the same colour as the background.) The page therefore broke Google's long-held rules on keyword stuffing and hidden text. It was lucky it was ranked as high as page 52.

Considering this example it's difficult to criticise Google's stance.

Testing

Modern Advertising is said to have been started by Claude Hopkins, who was successfully practising at the beginning of the twentieth century and was hugely successful. He wrote a book called 'Scientific Advertising' which was published in 1923 and is still available on Amazon. The backbone of his method was testing and keeping detailed notes of what worked and what didn't.

We're not saying that testing, recording the results and making inferences went out of fashion – but it was just another thing agencies were supposed to do and it wasn't top of anyone's list. Until internet marketing came along.

Internet marketers quickly realised that their new marketing offered the ability to test with instant feedback of stats at the touch of a button. Google AdWords even offers an A/B split testing facility within its AdGroups.

It's not just Google AdWords that benefits from testing; all aspects of internet marketing can and should be tested, tested and then tested again.

Testing marketing campaigns may have been developed 90-odd years ago but its disciples since have been low in numbers. Claude Hopkins was closely followed by John Caples's 'Tested Adverting Methods' but there has been little progress since then*. The first page of the first chapter of Caples's book has a few introductory lines, but half way down that first page is the first heading 'Two Classes of Advertising' and the two classes? 'The Testers' and 'The Non-Testers'.

A more modern advertising expert is David ('At 60 miles an hour the loudest noise in this new Rolls-Royce comes from the electric clock') Oglivy, but his 1983 book, 'Ogilvy on Advertising' mentions testing but doesn't really enthuse about it.

This modern reluctance is probably down to the cost of testing and the time it takes; modern budgeting and deadlines make advertisers and agencies balk at the prospect.

But IT changes all that. For a variety of reasons, all of which come down to the speed of the electron, testing in internet marketing is now easy, cheap and quick. Now there isn't a single successful internet marketer that claims good results without testing. Be prepared to have this point re-iterated again and again within this book and on our website – Claude Hopkins would have been proud of us and you owe it to yourself to continually test marketing campaigns because now you can – and cheaply and quickly.

*Caples was responsible for one of the most famous and enduring adverts of all time: 'They Laughed When I Sat Down At The Piano But When I Started To Play!' was a hugely copied headline but it was followed by four pages of copy to help its success as an advert and the achievements of the music school the advert was about. Testing and long copy have been used ever since. (Long copy does not mean simply padding out short copy until it becomes repetitious, boring and wasteful. It means taking the trouble to tell the whole story using as few words as possible.)

Our New Approach

There are too many tragedies of businesses 'trying' internet marketing and falling short.

How can that happen when Google AdWords has risen from nothing in less than ten years to become the most used advertising medium in the UK?

These are the answers to that question:

- Google AdWords cannot produce answers in isolation. You can't expect an advert restricted to 95 characters including spaces to do the job of creating interest, explaining benefits, answering objections and herding a prospect through a sales funnel to closing the sale and collecting the cash.
- A landing page (an effective one devoted to each keyword is essential to success) on a website won't attract attention. By its very nature a good one has all the charisma of a Single Issue Fanatic and would probably be penalised by Google for using duplicate copy.
- Emails however skilfully they are written and deployed need lots of good, qualified email addresses to be sent to, and you sure aren't going to get those off any shelf. (Doing so could easily lead to a ban for spamming.)

Try internet marketing with just one of those disciplines, as many do and have done, and it's just not going to work.

BUT, thinking about this conundrum brought the answer:

In isolation, they could bring patchy, even ordinary results.

But the whole is greater than the sum of its parts and the three disciplines together take on a new life. Outstripping previous performance the girder of Internet Marketing is held aloft by the three pillars of:

- Google AdWords
- Landing pages
- Well-designed email marketing campaigns

We work with our companion site PlannedSites.com to promote this New Approach. PlannedSites is so committed to this strategy that it will only work with clients that employ the Three-Pillar approach. PlannedSites might not be engaged by a client to do any website work or email work but it won't accept Google AdWords work without ensuring the website and the email aspects are properly in place. This is the same for the other Pillars. It's critical that internet marketing is carried out with this approach – and we won't complete any campaigns without it. We want to create campaigns that work and grow your profits and this is the only way to achieve your goals.

Internet marketing works. There is no doubt about that as Google AdWords is a billion dollar industry. It's also cost-effective, even inexpensive (you can't beat the cost of an email – nothing!), competes with the cost of direct mail, beats cold-calling prospects when they've just sat down to watch Corrie, is quick and flexible compared to traditional marketing, and pulverises television. radio and newspaper advertising on price.

The Three-Pillars approach works. It's the fastest and most devastating way to collect pin-point accurate prospects at a negligible cost – especially when you factor in the true value of your customers and your future prosperity.

We are eager to help and assist with your internet marketing objectives – and making sure you attain them. Apart from this book and our website we offer a free appraisal of your current internet marketing requirements – without obligation.

You may have already taken steps to start – but might not be achieving the results you anticipated. You may have tried to 'have a go' but abandoned the experiment after little or no success. No matter what level you are at or situation you are in we are sure we can help improve your results and take them to new levels of achievement and growth.

We've set up a special page on our site for you to take advantage of this FREE service. Please go to

www.plannedsites.com/FreeAppraisal

Imagine the profits you could be starting to multiply from TODAY if you obtained the vital help your business needs.

Sign up now - it's quick and easy!

Get a head start on competitors and see the difference expert help can make to your internet marketing campaign:

www.plannedsites.com/FreeAppraisal

Ray Griffin
rayg@plannedsites.com
Autumn 2014

Part One

I've divided the book into two sections to reflect the concept in the Introduction.

The first part is the essential ingredients of a successful internet marketing campaign – the three pillars.

The first three chapters reflect these three pillars and go into greater detail about the concepts.

Once you have mastered the three pillars you are ready to take your successful marketing campaign to a new level.

In Part Two we teach you the 'AfterBurners' – which include advanced techniques to keep you soaring above the competition.

Chapter 1: **Customers Come to You** – Google AdWords

Despite rumours you may have heard to the contrary Google AdWords is still unrivalled as an advertising medium. Facebook is making a brave fight of it as I write (and its rates are as competitive as AdWords were in its early days) but it can't get around the fact that Google AdWords is *pull* marketing (buyers looking for sellers) while Facebook will always be a traditional *push* environment (sellers looking for buyers).

How often do you randomly click on a product you were not looking for and buy it, as opposed to actively searching for a product or service you need? This is the obstacle Facebook has to overcome in getting you to click on an advert in the first place. And is the advantage Google has over other forms of internet marketing, such as banner ads, pop-ups and social media.

AdWords is the predominant advertising provider in the UK market (90%); it offers Display advertising, Ad extensions, Google Merchant Center, Mobile advertising and Remarketing, all within the same dashboard. Its unmatched tools include a Keyword Planner and an AdWords Editor. For the last year or two it has been the UK's biggest advertising medium measured by spend.

But there is no getting round the fact that Google AdWords is deceptively simple at first sight and Google is a bit naughty in exploiting that. 'Set up your free account and in ten minutes your first advert will be accessible by 100,000,000 people' is something they like to promote. What they don't tell you is that an advert set up like this, without any thought or prior background knowledge, is going to get you close to a 100% failure rate. Nor is Google forthcoming about the obvious fact that no-one in their right minds is going to start divulging their credit card details on a website they hadn't heard of five minutes previously.

Don't get me wrong – I'm a big fan of the Big G and dislike having to criticise it – but the truth remains; without in-depth knowledge or an enormous slice of luck, you're unlikely to be successful using Google AdWords straight out of the box.

Google AdWords *is* deceptively easy to use but there are so many of these easy parts the permutations and granular options to make vital decisions on are mind-blowing.

How the system works

You open up an account with Google AdWords and set up your first advert. The detail of the latter we'll go into on the website. Google places the advert onto its system and starts showing it on its SERPs (Search Engine Results' Pages) alongside the organic results (also known as the free listings). The organic results take up most of the main content area to the left. At the top and to the right hand side are smaller listings; these are the paid adverts.

The searcher is now presented with a screen showing 21 items. He will read them and click on what matches his search term best. It could be a free listing or it could be a paid advert. Whatever it is, the searcher is taken to the relevant website.

When a searcher clicks on your advert Google charges you (hence the term 'Pay-Per-Click' or 'PPC'). The important stat here is the Click-Through-Rate or CTR, the percentage of clicks against the number of times the advert was shown. CTRs are used by you as a measure of success and by Google as a factor in its calculation of Quality Score (there is more on this one the website (www.plannedsites.com)). This is the most important Pay-Per-Click stat of them all as it can affect your advert's position, how much discount Google gives you and how much you will be charged.

Achieving click-throughs is what Google AdWords is all about and many AdWords' professionals see that as the end of their job. Marketers, though, will be aware that the job is not finished until there is cash in the bank, the real stats being conversion rate and ROI – return on investment. How many potential customers sign-up or buy a product is the only way to evaluate the success of an AdWords campaign.

Devising a successful AdWords strategy

Keywords

In the land of websites, keywords are the words searchers use to find things on Google. For example type 'Morphy Richards kettle' into Google to find, yep, you've guessed it, a Morphy Richards kettle. SERPs are pages of search results that Google presents a searcher in response to his search term. Unfortunately we don't call them search terms, we call them keywords. Search terms is often a more accurate way to describe modern web searches. It's rare just to have someone search for one or two words anymore; Google often brings back too many search results and more and more searchers are using very specific phrases and descriptions to find exactly what they are looking for. But for the purposes of sticking to what Google AdWords uses, we will continue to use 'keywords'.

Keywords are important for optimising a website for prominent showings in the SERPs. The same keywords are equally important in Google AdWords whose adverts share a SERP with the organic listings. When setting up an advert we have to tell Google which keyword(s) should cause our advert to show.

A keyword can be any number of words long and searchers use four-word keywords more than one-word keywords.

Thorough keyword research is critical. Google matches keywords to the adverts offered by advertisers; when they match then, and only then, can the advert be displayed. Get your keyword research wrong and your advert is not going to be displayed to your intended audience.

We can help with all aspects of keyword research. It is a complex subject but the pay-off is discovering how your customers *really* search to find your products and services. With thorough keyword research you can also find hidden keyword gems – those with low competition and low costs. To learn more, view:

www.plannedsites.com/KeywordResearch

Adverts

Your advert only has one job; to gain the searcher's click when he has 21 choices on the SERP. Images aren't allowed, so it's down to the magic of words and you have precious few of them. Your allowance is 95 *characters* including spaces and a headline.

The key to success is an empathy with a searcher's needs. Keep in mind at all times that the advert's job is solely to gain that precious click. You're NOT trying to sell anything at this stage.

Landing page

All sites on a SERP are waiting eagerly for the searcher's decision and the click that brings victory – but only victory in that individual battle. The winning of the war, ultimately, is the satisfying increase of profit as your bank account is swelled by the steady stream of orders generated by your campaign.

Landing pages, the pre-determined destinations of the clicks are the next important step and are considered in the next chapter.

For now, Google AdWords has delivered the precious click-through to your landing page – so it's job is done, until next time.

Relevancy

I can't emphasise enough the amount of importance Google gives to relevancy. If your keyword/advert/landing page combination do not rate highly for relevancy you're a non-starter.

Don't imagine that there is a roomful of Googlers in California poring over adverts and landing pages and comparing them to each other and to their keywords for relevancy. Googlers are cleverer than that.

They've written an algorithm to do the work for them. No-one except Google insiders knows what it says or how it works. What I can tell you is that when I've looked at a client's AdWords, and checked the adverts that have been rated low for relevancy by Google, they have indeed been lacking in suitable keywords. I can't argue with it.

Don't be tempted into thinking that a random Google staffer is unfairly penalising your advert. It's not a subjective finding, it's based on tried and tested algorithms that stick to cold hard facts. So if Google says you fall down on relevancy, you fall down on relevancy. Put it right and move on.

Where do you go now?

This is a good news/bad news dilemma.

The bad news is that either you or one or more of your colleagues either have to spend considerable time, energy and money on learning the minutiae and expertise required to run Google AdWords (not forgetting the keyword research you would have to do, in order to make sure you were targeting the right keywords, at the right price) or you pay us to run a guaranteed, expert, money generating campaign for you.

The good news is that when you decide to embrace Google AdWords you are employing the greatest advertising revolution in marketing's long history, now occupying top slot in the list of the UK's profit driving advertising channels.

You have total (minute-by-minute) control over your advertising, its budget, its reach and its scheduling. It's the ultimate in selling and creating targeted customers; its basic philosophy of bringing buyers to sellers means you never address an unqualified prospect again. No more running after potential (often disinterested shoppers) and losing precious resources to time wasters. Let the willing buyers come to you.

Chapter 2: **Talk to Prospects, Person to Person** – Landing Pages doing their proper job

Landing pages are the pages on our websites to which we take visitors when we want to guide them to specific content.

In this context we are talking about the landing pages we use in our Google AdWords campaigns, the pages prospects see when they click through, the moment when your Google account gets debited.

But landing pages can also be important for email links or references in magazine or newspaper articles. The ultimate landing page is, of course, the Home page - but we never use that for Google AdWords landing pages, and I hope that is obvious by the time you get to the end of this chapter.

When landing pages were becoming fashionable they were sniffed at a bit by Google and the Google community, rather like tradesmen used to be when applying to join exclusive golf clubs.

This initial scepticism and reserve about landing pages has now been forgotten. Creation, design and writing of landing page content is now a specialised discipline. I have a 368-page tome on my bookshelves entitled 'Landing Page Optimization'. (It's as dry as it sounds, I can assure you.)

Google now encourages the pursuit of landing page excellence and provides a tool for optimising landing pages. Essentially it offers A/B testing facilities for two or more choices of landing page design or content.

Special Googlebot

Robots are computer programs roaming the internet. Sometimes called crawlers or spiders, they wander from site to site gathering information along the way. There is nothing to stop any company writing its own robot to spy on competitors. The robot that Google uses to index the pages on the billions of sites around the world is predictably called the Googlebot.

Google also has a specialist Googlebot for examining landing pages when they are deployed in Google AdWords.

Before going into details on this specialist Googlebot it is worth emphasising Google's underlying philosophy so that we understand what's going on. Top of Google's list of priorities is that its users have a great online experience. Users are top of the list, argues Google, because they are the ones who are critical to everything and everybody connected to Google – its customers, shareholders and employees. No satisfied users, no Google. So the Googlebot that spiders landing pages will be ranking user friendly-pages much higher.

This Googlebot examines the landing page first to compare relevancy with the keywords and the advert that is sending visitors to it. It also assesses page quality – structure, design and content. But it also examines the website behind the landing page. It has, of course, its own assessment of the site from the standard Googlebot which is designed to assess websites from a different perspective. The landing page Googlebot wants to know the site is a substantial contributor to its purported subject and fits in with the keywords and advert.

If, for example, the site was trying to push a pyramid selling scheme (of which Google frowns on anyway) and the keywords and adverts were in alliance with the landing page in deceiving the user, it would take a poor view. Really deceptive and underhand sites have their AdWords accounts closed.

The landing page element of the three-pillar structure has to take into account the whole site, not just the landing page itself.

Landing Page structure, design and content

A landing page has to handle a precious commodity (your prospect visiting your page), in such a delicate and balanced way that you do not lose them to poor layout, poor content or lack of trust in the site itself.

We have worked very hard to get that click. Not only that but we must also realise that its monetary value is more than the cost-per-click that AdWords is charging us for.

If we achieve a 10% conversion rate, then one user coming through to the landing page on a click costing £5 will feature in our costings as £5 x 10 = £50.

To put even more pressure on ourselves we must also take into account that we will have calculated elsewhere (Chapter 14 – Value of a Customer) that a client is worth £630 (when we consider the lifetime value of a particular customer).

So the click has cost £50 and if we don't convert it the cost will be increased by the loss of a prospective asset worth £630. If those doesn't give you incentive to create a page that converts – nothing will!

The first issue is that the visitor, like every other visitor on every other website, is twitchy.

Just some of the questions they might be thinking when they arrive at your landing page, could be:

- Is this what I'm looking for?
- Am I wasting my time?
- Can I trust this site?
- Do they sound like they know what they're talking about?

The first finger on his right hand, having just clicked to get through to the site is poised to click a second time – but this time with the mouse pointer hovering over the Back button. If he does, kiss goodbye to money you've spent on Google AdWords, and any future profits you could have made from this customer.

How can we make the first impression positive? It's actually quite easy, but most landing pages get it wrong and over-complicate matters – but for now, let's incorporate some useful pointers:

- Keep your page clean and uncluttered – use white space to draw attention to the areas you wish visitors to read.
- Don't confuse the reader with a multitude of links – including navigation bars – which are easy temptations for the visitor to investigate other parts of your website with the constant risk of losing the prospect altogether.

The second thing is the page heading. This should be the visitor's search term and your keyword. Top left of the content area, big and bold, so it can't be missed.

At this point the back button will be less of a pull to the visitor.

The banner looks professionally designed and there is his search term right smack in his eye line. Even the most wary punter will concede that things are looking good in his quest to find what he was looking for.

You must consider what your user is looking for. If they search for a camera you need to know where the visitor is in your sales funnel. A sales funnel is simply a concept designed to work out where your customers are in their intentions to buy. Top of the funnel, for instance, would be a low level of awareness about a product, but wanting to find out more. Bottom of the sales funnel, is a 'handing over the cash; gotta have this product right now' moment.

A search term of 'camera' probably means 'I'm at the beginning and I'm doing some research'. Talk to him in that way, in broad terms with more background information. Concede to yourself that this is NOT going to be a sale, at least on this visit, but do everything to put your site at the top of the visitor's list of helpful sites he could eventually buy from.

A search for 'SLR camera' will probably mean 'I've narrowed my search a little so please tell me more about this category' so talk to him in *that* way – greater detail on SLR cameras and the information required to know what type of SLR he's after.

.
   A 'Nikon D3100 14.2MP DSLR Camera with 18-55mm Lens – Black' keyword is a definite 'I've made up mind, I want to buy this specific model'. Your landing page this time could well be your product page – as long as it follows the

rules of landing page content especially regarding links. Whatever you're doing make sure you're empathising with your visitor. You could well be competing purely on price at this stage, so you need to be getting into the habit of thinking about what advantages you can offer your customer to swing that sale to you.

Dealing with a newcomer to your website

Put yourself in the newcomer's shoes and let's change the camera theme. Let's say your site is selling clothes and the searcher has used 'blue sweater' as a search term.

The prospect has just arrived on your 'blue sweater' landing page. He's never seen it before. He's never been on the site before. He's never even heard of it.

Back to the site-owner and consider the his thoughts: how am I going to get this guy to make a purchase when he knows absolutely zilch about me and my site?

You don't have to be a genius to work out that your're just not going to do that. Never mind in a month of Sundays; it isn't going to happen in a lifetime of Sundays.

What do you do?

You do something achievable; you start building a relationship with the prospect. Instead of you trying to sell him something you give him something. It has to be of a recognisable value, and truly worth time and effort. The practical thing is something in writing or a video, something that can be emailed to him.

As he used the search term 'blue sweater' you could send him your whitepaper 'How to Double the Life of a Sweater'. The whitepaper has got to be more than 'wash in warm soapy water'. It has to be a multi-page pdf, use illustrations, and be original in your content and make it useful – give value to the customer!

Whatever your offer is, provide a form on the landing page by which you send him the PDF. This will give you his email address and then you're away.

Away? Where? How?

The email is the very core of all internet marketing systems and will probably remain so even if someone finds a way of charging for it. It is one of the important innovations of the last fifty years. Properly handled it will transform your business and keep you ahead of your competitors.

That is why I said at the end of the last section: 'This form will give you his email address, and then you're away'. You see, the whole point of giving value to the customer in the first place was, in return, to receive that prized email address.

Now you've got it, you can woo your prospect with everything you know about the world of blue sweaters for many a long day, cultivating a relationship that should reap rewards for years.

The landing page, having done the hard work of gaining the email address, can take a well-earned break.

We can now hand over to the world of exploiting email marketing systems – using them to create profit and long lasting customer growth, like you never before imagined.

Chapter 3: **Exploit the Miracle of FREE Communications** – email campaigns that work

Back in the mists of time when I was a callow youth slowly emerging into maturity the culture I occupied (if you can occupy a culture) was quite clear on its attitude to Direct Mail. It didn't work. It was an utter waste of time. It was a misuse of paper. It all went straight into the dustbin.

But I was an inquisitive individual and it began to dawn on me that I was giving lip-service to an unproved 'fact' of life, that Direct Mail was all rubbish and wasn't worth the paper it was printed on. In my arrogant way I thought that if I was to go on endorsing this part of my culture I should start some exploration and at least decide for myself the true worth of Direct Mail.

At the time I was training to be an accountant and my work was almost solely confined to small businesses in the local area. I asked them if they ever used Direct Mail. Their replies were unanimous in their contempt of the medium. I was no further on. But the junk mail (as it came to be called) kept coming and I became more convinced that I was still a long way from the truth.

After qualifying as an accountant, I moved to London for a few years (it was the done thing in those days) and worked for a City firm. Their clients included bigger clients and I was assigned to an audit of a company that actually used Direct Mail. Not only that but it used Christian Brann's company as its Direct Mail contractor.

Some readers of this book won't have heard of Christian Brann nor the magazine he made famous – Reader's Digest. But back then, Reader's Digest was a household name. Millions of homes used to subscribe to the magazine and it was delivered by post. Marketing was fulfilled by Direct Mail. Brann was the brains behind the campaigns. He pioneered what Microsoft now calls MailMerge. Recipients would receive a pre-printed letter with their names (obviously over-printed afterwards as insertion techniques were primitive) in the salutation – but there would be another obvious overprint in the middle of the letter referring to the area in which they lived, usually the county extracted from the address, in order to make the letter seem even more personal. It was blatantly artificial BUT IT WORKED.

As I was in charge of the audit, I decided I needed to make a trip to see Brann's company as part of the audit programme. My earlier curiosity about Direct Mail was satisfied upon meeting Brann himself, the acclaimed national authority on Direct Mail, and it was a real eye-opener. He was a driven individual but enormously personable.

The answers I had been seeking all those years were:

1. Direct Mail is a success if it brings a mere 1% response. Which accounts for why so much seems to

be thrown away. It IS binned - but one in a hundred is responded to first.

2. The aim of Direct Mail is NOT to sell whatever it says on the day-glow envelope but to gather names and addresses of the elusive 1% so they can be sold other products and services in the future. This produces a list of 'double' value:

(a) selling to the individuals again and
(b) selling the list itself to other companies.

The enterprise's profit lies in exploiting the list in these ways, not in the immediate sale.

Thanks for sticking with me on the Direct Mail marketing lesson from the days of Reader's Digest – but history is repeating itself. (And you know what they say about not learning lessons from history.)

Heard any of these?:

- Email doesn't work
- Email's obsolete
- Never open them
- Shouldn't be allowed

and many other excuses for not using it.

Email's similarity with Direct Mail is uncanny. They are on parallel paths.

So, please listen to me when I tell you that email will be the most important part of your internet marketing life and therefore the most important part of the future of your business IF ONLY YOU WILL LET IT. You just have to understand that and take on board:

1. The effect Christian Brann had on Reader's Digest and its spin-offs (and when he retired Reader's Digest went into decline – he was that influential).
2. You and your competitors are looking for a breakthrough in your field to get the advantage over one another. Whoever fully embraces email first in your niche will give themselves an unassailable lead.

Let's refresh ourselves on what email can do:

Using email marketing you can send a personalised email, with many options and tailored choices to fit exactly who you are talking to – many more than Christian Brann had (for example, videos and links to other web pages), across the globe to 10,000 people at the touch of a button; have it read by them immediately and for FREE. And follow it up for FREE. And follow up the follow-up for FREE.

Why would you ever turn down this opportunity? You can bet one of your competitors won't if you do.

It doesn't make any sense not to maximise this amazing opportunity NOW– especially as there'll be someone, somewhere who'll eventually figure out a way of charging for it.

Maybe the reluctance to use it is because you've used it in the past without success – or your competitors aren't making much headway either.

It's something we put as a top priority. to make every single email campaign count. So much so that at least 30% of our time is spent on researching the latest marketing trends and strategies that work and you can keep out-performing your rivals. You'll find more on this later in the book and on our website.

Email is the only way of being able to keep in touch with

your prospects and customers. (Correction – it's not the only way, but the alternatives would involve printing thousands of mail shots, paying for designers and postage, or cold calling all day and running up huge phone bills).

Exploiting email to the full you'll learn, among dozens of things:

- Provided you've followed all the rules and guidelines we show you, you can't send too many emails
- If you think you aren't sending enough emails and using them fully, then your business is creeping towards out-moded practices and in extreme cases extinction
- How to use your customer email database. This will be made up of information and data you have gathered in order to enhance and zero in on prospects (don't worry, it's not the massive investment the word 'database' can sometimes mean, in fact it's free and in the cloud)
- Your email database will shortly become your most valuable asset, second only to the main list of contacts itself.
- Your email department (you didn't know you were setting up a separate department, did you?) will become your best business friend.

Finally . . . . a word on salesmanship and trickery

In Britain 'selling' is not on, a bit below the belt, not the done thing. Introducing yourself at a party as a sales person can be the social kiss of death.

There's no rhyme or reason to this prejudice – and it's time to face the facts. And it matters to us, here, because having email as part of your marketing repertoire is seen by some as the same sort of black art as selling itself.

Selling is not forcing yourself on someone against their will, or tricking them into buying a service or product they do not want or need. Selling is not the equivalent of the five-card trick.

Selling is quite simply the exchange between two willing parties of a product or service for an agreed sum of money. The buyer and the seller are both willing parties. More than that the buyer WANTS the product or service, or he wouldn't part with the money to buy it in the first place. Obviously the seller wants to sell it or it wouldn't be for sale.

The law of the land regarding internet marketing (called the Distance Selling Regulations in the UK) includes safeguards against crooks, of course; the same law protects the buyer if the goods aren't as he expected which can happen when only a photograph is available. The law requires the seller fully to refund a buyer who returns goods within seven days, *for whatever reason.*

We can go further. If the buyer wants the product or service – and we have what he wants to buy – it is our moral duty to let him know we have that service or product available and at the best value. Not doing this could mean that the customer goes away looking for the nearest alternative, even if it is inferior to the one you are currently offering.

In our tutorials you will learn how to create an email that will greatly increase the chance of your prospect opening and reading it. There is no room for boring, run-of-the mill or un-professional emails that have not been thought out properly. Time is precious, and you have a small window of opportunity to make your emails count. You also owe it to yourself and customer to make them aware of your product, especially as you might be the only source of it. (Becoming an only source, in other words creating a genuine USP is covered in Chapter 9.)

The third pillar

Email rightly takes its place as the third and perhaps mightiest of our three-pillar system to ensure your internet marketing success.

Long live FREE email. Take advantage of this massive income driving powerhouse while you can. Your business can't afford not to.

Part Two

I've divided the book into two sections to reflect the central concept in the Introduction.

The second part is the AfterBurners.

I showed in the Introduction how the three-pillar approach to your internet marketing was essential to success. I went on to explain that, having established a successful system, you should then look for further effective techniques to lift yourself to the next level.

The AfterBurners here are not comprehensive. There are many more. But I've included the most efficient and time effective methods to get you off to a flying start.

The ones I have selected cover most aspects of what you would need. They are each stand-alone; they are not interdependent like the three-pillars.

Chapter 4: **Putting Your Stats in their Proper Place** – Focus on Your Goal

Internet marketing gives you many opportunities to take your eye off the ball. That's apart from the human tendency to take the path of least resistance and go for the easy opportunity or quick win.

Internet marketing's a discipline of many parts and one of its big advantages (and disadvantages!) is the ability to access lots of reports and stats which can distract you. It is difficult to interpret data correctly, with lots of noise and short-term apparent patterns obscuring the underlying trends and confusing your objectives.

Whatever your method of marketing there is only one goal and it's increasing the bank balance. Nothing else matters. So anything that either doesn't achieve it or diminishes it is out. But a snag is that there are waypoints leading to your final goal. They are important in getting us there and shouldn't be ignored but a waypoint isn't increasing profit.

One such waypoint is the click-through-rate (CTR) of an Google AdWord advert. We use it to:

- compare last week's clicks with this week's

- to help Quality Score
- to work out percentage of conversions
- to test ads or keywords
- to measure the success or weakness of whoever is conducting our campaign

And in the last point there is a trap for the unwary. The conductor of an Adwords' campaign has an incentive not to achieve maximum conversions but to achieve maximum CTR. He even has an incentive to maximise the CTR at the expense of conversions particularly if his income is affected. Clicks obtained in this way may not only affect the number of sales, they could have an adverse effect on your business. You are going to have to pay for all those extra clicks (mostly irrelevant and sometimes misleading) and your prospect is not going to be happy with a page that does not meet her needs. Why would they return to your site if the landing page was such a disappointment in the first place?

There are similar hazards in landing pages. Are the benefits of the product overstated so that the page's author can achieve more downloads?

The email segment is another with its own set of stats and data. These include:

- Delivery rate of emails
- Open rate of emails
- And its own click through rate from links in the content.

Admittedly the factors affecting delivery rate won't be much to do with conversion rate but concentrating energy on it at the expense of more productive adjustments is not a good idea.

These disciplines are different from one another and tend to be the responsibility of different people with different skills, some in-house and some outside contractors. Included are the web developers apparently doing their best to make a mockery of the landing page wireframe (a basic plan of your web page and navigation). Their skills are not to make you money or maximise your conversion rates but to ensure your pages look nice; they don't seem to care what your marketing aims are or how extra links will merely leak prospects to other parts of your site. You need to be able to educate them in the importance of your marketing objectives, and make sure they are fully on board with YOUR targets. If a developer is putting the coding of menus before making you money … you need to find yourself a new web developer.

There needs to be a strong leader of this disparate crew, a leader who understands that only one achievement matters – increasing your bank balance.

Finally the best result is not necessarily represented by the size of the statistic. Take CTR – do you want ten clicks from tyre kickers who appreciated the humour in the headline but couldn't care less for your message or five clicks from serious prospects all of whom downloaded your whitepaper?

Remove the possibility that individuals working for you may be 'improving' their stats at the cost of steering your campaign away from excellent leads that on first glance appear to be smaller in number and, and for that reason only, less impressive. Quality of prospects beats volume every time.

Chapter 5: **Making it Easy for your Customers** – Usability (or UX)

Google set out its stall early on in its life (it's only fifteen years old anyway). It wanted 'to create a great user experience' and that is still its declared ambition but it goes further and states that users are top of the category list labeled 'important' above advertisers, investors and employees. Users, it argues, must have a great experience for the latter categories' well-being and future prosperity.

UX is short for UXD which stands for User Experience Design. Here we'll just refer to it as UX as the rest of the website world does.

Businesses don't usually get involved much in this subject leaving it to web developers or designers. Unless you are employing a top-quality developer and paying him top dollar that almost certainly means your website is average at best.

Our aim is to lift you permanently above average in all areas. It's the only place to be.

Before you launch into full blown UX, you have to learn how to test your site correctly – Usability Testing.

Usability Testing

Under usability testing a website is tested for its structure, visual design and user experience by random testers who are new to the site and subject. They are paid a small fee for an hour of their time. A supervisor asks questions and sets tasks which are designed to find issues and difficulties with the site. For instance, you may have used jargon or technical language that is understood within your company but lost on your visitors.

A developer may have created what he thinks is an innovative menu system but if users find it difficult to use it's going to lose and confuse his audience.

Usability testing is not popular with your average Yellow Pages website developer because of either fear of failure (ridiculous if you rightly regard failure as a route to success) or inferred criticism (in which case they ought to have thought of it first). So the canny business builds usability testing in to the project from the beginning – especially if he's read this book.

Testing sessions should take place regularly during site development and start as early as possible though late testing is better than no testing at all.

Testing shouldn't be a big deal. If it is you've over-complicated the process. Three tests in a morning (preferably with new testers each time) conducted by a supervisor who knows what he's doing (it doesn't take an Einstein to get it right but hit-and-miss procedures will invalidate the process.) These tests can be recorded with software that tracks clicks and mouse movements.

Share the results with the team over a sandwich at lunch-time and the job's a good 'un. You'll be both amazed and humbled by the results:

- amazed because of the improvements to comprehension, clicks and content,
- humbled as a result of finding obvious mistakes that can impede performance and use of your website.

It's not too late if your site has already launched, particularly if it's not bringing in the results you were hoping for.

Test the whole site – which may take several mornings of three tests each. Leave at least a day between tests to take action to implement findings before moving onto the next area to test.

I guarantee you will be staggered at the improvement you can make on your pages and save time and money on high bounce rates.

UX – the professional angle

UX comes in three parts:

1. Graphic design
2. Software
3. Interactivity

Each of these areas of expertise demands its own dedicated professionals and they need to work as a team to bring better results. That fact alone means it's a discipline beyond the reach of most businesses that have to rely on their own people or on this book and its associated website for advice and guidance.

Graphic design

There are rules of composition and balance that have to be followed to help with the overall design and harmony of the site. Graphic designers also make use of extensive research into eye-movement and user interest within a page to determine where the most important pieces of information should be located.

There are a number of no-nos to be avoided as well. An example is the request for information that has no apparent relevance to an online form. Traditional marketing people try to insist that a telephone number be a required field in a form when it isn't necessary. Nothing riles a user more than this sort of irritation. It's a good way to make your customers waste time, question why you need all these details and you lose goodwill.

Horizontal scroll-bars are also the enemy of usability. Do anything, anything at all, to avoid them.

Software

The programmers need to follow best practice as well as making the whole package seamless and easy to use. In former times (well, only a few years ago, actually) some sites would tell you that you'd made an error in filling in a form and then delight in deleting everything that had been correctly entered, making you start from scratch. This is a great way to annoy and lose customers.

Interactivity

Using form-filling as an example again, the team member in charge of content should be wary of presenting a huge form. Some ignorant content developers produce pages with so many boxes to complete that a vertical scroll bar is needed. Nothing deters visitors like a never-ending ladder of empty boxes to complete. Two tips you can implement today:

1. Break up the screen into two or more pages

2. Employ a postcode-driven address finder so that addresses can be completed automatically from the entry of a postcode. The service is cheap enough to run – only a few pence per entry and can earn you money by keeping customers focused long enough to complete the form.

Chapter 6: **Have Your Customers Tell You What They Want** – Testing

Advertising testing first came into marketers' firmament when Claude Hopkins, a copywriter of the early nineteenth century who worked in a big New York advertising agency, published a book called 'Scientific Advertising' in 1923, ninety-one years ago.

The really remarkable thing about this book is you can still buy it on Amazon (and presumably elsewhere) and it's available as a Kindle book. Amazon seems ashamed that it is old and gives more than one recent publishing date on its website. Don't believe them. The book, as I say, is called 'Scientific Advertising' by Claude Hopkins. You can test authenticity by looking at the table of contents. Chapter 1 is called 'How Advertising Laws Are Established'.

Many modern marketers are proud to own and to have read the book – me included. It is, in fact, on my desk at the moment. There are only 82 pages in it and it's a good read. I wouldn't dare admit how many times I've read it. But the fascinating thing is that so many marketers still refer to it today.

Getting back to the main point – Claude invented advertising testing and there is no better way of putting his point across than reproducing the first three paragraphs of Chapter Fifteen – Test Campaigns:

'Almost any question can be answered, cheaply, quickly and finally by a test campaign. And that's the way to answer them – not by arguments around a table. Go the court of last resort – the buyers of your product.

'On every new project there comes up the question for selling the article profitably. You and your friends may like it, but the majority may not. Some rival product may be better liked or cheaper. It may be strongly entrenched. The users won away from it may cost too much to get.

'People may buy and not repeat. The article may last too long. It may appeal to a small percentage, so most of your advertising goes to waste.'

What's out of date about that information?

And, as I don't have the impudence to try and improve them, take them as my first three paragraphs of this chapter, too.

I only need add what modern methods, that weren't available to Claude, can add:

1. Speed. In the 1920s testing was completed by collecting the coupons clipped from newspapers, catalogues and magazines. The adverts would have to be planned and written carefully as the subsequent actions to turn them into messages on a printed page were so laborious. Printing blocks would need to be made (one for each publication as a unique code would need to be incorporated so the publication could be identified) and sent to the publishers in adequate time. The actual publication could add weeks to the process. Google AdWords

adverts can be written and published to 100,000,000 potential website visitors in a few minutes. Claude refers to 'cheaply and quickly' in the first sentence to this chapter. He would be green with envy at what we can achieve today.

2.   Collating the results. Today Google AdWords presents us with automatically prepared reports, the ability to customise our own reports and we put the results into spreadsheets for analysis. Claude had a blank piece of paper to work on.

3.   Things to test: we can and should test everything we can so that we are getting the biggest bang for our buck. The only reason to stop extending testing is finding something with more potential to test.

With a little imagination you can find all sorts of things to test:

a.   As I write this, we are preparing to use Google AdWords to test our website tagline

b.   You can also use Google AdWords to do market research and test the marketability of a new invention BEFORE you go to the expense of production.

See how these are done:

www.plannedsites.com/LateralAdwords

The discouraging thing about the subject of testing is that so many people just give lip service to it. Successful marketers are testing all the time.

Be wise and follow the money.

Chapter 7: **More Profits in Less Time – 80/20**; Pareto's Gift to You – Extreme Profitability and Elevated Productivity

[In the Acknowledgements at the start of this book you will have gathered that I think rather a lot of my editor. During numerous discussions and conversations (when she never got ratty with me, though surely provoked) she revealed she not only knew *of* 80/20 but actually knew *it*. Probably better than me. So I asked her to contribute this chapter as author and here it is, the one chapter in this book that hasn't been (or had to be) edited.]

Chapter 7: **More Profits in Less Time – 80/20;** Pareto's Gift to You – Extreme Profitability and Elevated Productivity

by Gail Watson

In 1906, Italian economist Vilfredo Pareto noticed **that 80% of Italy's land was owned by just 20% of the people.** Examined further, these **20% of land owners held 80%** of the wealth as well.

Intrigued by this finding, Pareto studied further and discovered that this law seemed to apply to many diverse subjects and areas.

From town sizes to wine production, to farm and field yields to stock growths in the financial markets, these laws still applied. Eventually he became obsessed with the pea plants growing in his garden, when he found (yep, you guessed it) 80% of peas came from just 20% of the plants.

This law not only applied to strict financial markets and banking sectors, but to plants, animals and people. It was an overriding natural law that seemed to affect everything he came to examine.

Even in your day-to-day life you will find:

- 80% of your phone calls will be to 20% of your contacts
- 80% of the benefit from fitness training can be found from 20% of the exercises carried out
- 80% of time spent dining out will be at your favourite 20% of restaurants

Why the 80/20 Principle is the Most Important Principle Your Business Can Learn Today

At this point you're probably thinking, interesting facts and story but how does a long dead economist from Italy, farm size and plant yields apply to my business, here, today?

Well, just focusing on your business alone you will find:

- 80% of all income will come from just 20% of your customers
- 80% of all web traffic will mainly come from 20% of sources

On the flip side, you will also discover:

- 80% of customer complaints will come from the same 20% of customers

- 80% of productivity will come from 20% of your actions

These statistics are just the tip of the Pareto iceberg - with 80% knowledge being hidden.

There are numerous ways you can find value and advantage once you are taught how to discover them. Even learning can be broken down into its component parts to accelerate understanding.

As incredible as that information is, it gets even more astonishing when you discover there are **hidden Power Laws** that exist within **the top 20% of results.**

For example, you will find that 80% of all traffic uses 20% of the roads. But within that top 20% you will find a further 20% can be applied to the original 20%.

That means 64% of traffic will be using just 4% of all roads.

And if you examine these figures further they just keep on going … until they reach saturation point – 41% of drivers will use just 0.2% of those roads (we're probably talking about the M1 at rush hour).

Power Laws and How They Can Advance Your Business

Applying this theory to your customers, you'll find that within the top 20% there are customers willing to buy other products and services from you at an increased price. These products also have to be of increased value of course – but the value to you of knowing how these value equations work is immearurable.

Instead of constantly chasing new clients and customers, wasting money on advertisements you may not need, you can focus all your attention on those golden top 20%. You are maximising the benefit to this exclusive club, while growing profits and earnings for your company.

Within the top 20% there will be another prime 4% (20% of the top 20%) who will buy even more.

Unlocking these secret Power Laws is what is going to keep you in business, but not just getting along, head-above-water survival. This is outstripping your rivals and leaving them in your wake. The only thing that will slow you down is your willingness to examine the areas of your business that will benefit from these principles.

This rule applies to EVERYTHING within your business:

- Analysing Google AdWords to find the adverts that produce the best ROI
- What channels of advertising are getting low response rates

These are just a couple of the ways the 80/20 Principle can help you today. It really is only limited by the amount of effort and observation you put into it. But like anything of value in life, you have to learn the principles thoroughly and accurately.

Genius as Michelangelo was, he could never have painted the Sistine Chapel if he had not first mastered the tools of his trade. Become a master of the Pareto Principle and the world is yours to be treasured and understood.

Small Actions – Massive Outcomes

When you realise that small actions can have exponential growth, you will look at everything differently. Small pivot points can be opened up to lever massive advancement and profit – not to mention the amount of time and money that can be saved from these actions.

Every day will become an exciting quest to search out new and exceptional ways of accomplishing your dreams – with less waste, more money, and increased time to spare to achieve astronomical outcomes.

Chapter 8: **Banish the Soothsayers – SEO – RIP**

The most notorious acronym in internet marketing has been administered the last rites. With Google acting as judge, jury and executioner.

SEO could well have earned the most consultancy fees in the short history of the World Wide Web. I haven't done the research and I doubt the figures exist.

Many can't believe it. Judging by the forums many don't believe it, or there are enough SEO 'specialists' still trying to frighten website owners into worrying themselves sick over the latest Penguin or Panda updates.

Let's go back and see what we're talking about. First, two acronyms – SEO stands for Search Engine Optimisation (or the art of making a web page climb to the top of the search engine rankings) and SERP stands for Search Engine Results' Page.

Google is the centre of everything here. Before Google there were search engines, certainly. But they didn't show sites in any meaningful order; juggling of links and title pages (even when not remotely relevant) was common practice.

Google had its revolutionary method of sorting sites according to their popularity. Factors it took into consideration were:

- How many links from other sites pointed to your site?
- What was the quality and relevance of the websites who passed on the links to your web pages?

Google gave the world the search engine it wanted (ranking websites by popularity and usefulness) but a beast was simultaneously born; this untamed beast was the throng of SEO consultants who offered you the chance (if you paid enough) of reaching the top of the SERPs results.

The new consultants gleaned whatever information they could from Google's press releases and video updates about improved search results and updates to Google's search algorithm. The best the SEO consultants could offer was educated guesses, at worst misleading advice that could damage your rankings and standing within Google.

Inadvertently Google had lit the fire and then piled fuel on top of it.

SEO consultants soon multiplied and sprouted from every corner of the web, spreading the message far and wide that they could get you on the hallowed Google first page spot, if you had enough cash – and were prepared to keep on paying to stay there. I was one of them so who am I to talk?

As is obvious now, two important factors are at work here:

1. Google started it
2. Only Google could stop it.

It took Google a long time to realise they had to do something. SEO had become artificial and untrustworthy. I remember advising on a sports website based in the Midlands whose cricket equipment category page had the word 'cricket' mentioned over 160 times on a rather small page. Because of the repeat of the word 'cricket' the page made no sense at all. To be fair Google had warned that the practice of 'keyword stuffing' would be penalised.

Google realised that website owners and developers had been abusing meta tags (a meta tag is a hidden area on web pages that allows you write what the page is about, without it being seen by the general reader but still allowing a Googlebot to 'read' it). With Google announcing it was now going to ignore keyword meta tags, developers and SEO consultants simply dumped the keywords onto the main content page for everyone to have to plough through.

Another problem was the philosophy on links. A link is the mechanism by which HTML (the programming language which drives the world wide web) takes a website visitor from one site to another. With their work on links at the end of the nineties Google's founders ranked websites into order according to the strength of the links to it.

Google developed their ranking system but they always clung on to the links part of the algorithm as the most important part despite the much better measurements they'd developed. You could understand the sentimental attachment. But it led to the horrifying phenomenon of link farms – websites that blatantly offered to create dozens of links.

Other areas were also found to exploit and manipulate by the SEO consultants. It all had to stop.

Google now says you have to create a website that gives the user a good experience. Content has to be relevant and original. Sites should always be kept up-to-date. It doesn't like duplicate copy so retailers who merely copy and paste their suppliers' catalogues aren't poplar, and can be downgraded by Google. It likes blogs (because new content is appearing all the time) and social media (particularly Google+) which will probably replace links in Google's approval ratings.

All this doesn't mean we have to throw the baby out with the bathwater. Links will still get you a boost in the rankings if they are relevant and from an authoritative site. Keywords should still appear in the right places - headers, meta descriptions (still used for SERPs snippets – so make these readable and interesting so that customers would want to click and learn more) but, above all, the content has to be original and relevant. Google implores us to write content for our visitors and not for Google, which, essentially, was what SEO was all about.

A point for the future is the changing face of SERPs. The eagle-eyed will have spotted changes in recent times. The free listings are losing ground to the adverts.

The latter took over the area at the top of the free listings some time ago and now regularly occupy the top three slots. These adverts are given more space than of old with the very top one sometimes given what Google calls site extensions – in effect free links to up to six more pages on the advertiser's site. There are other features in this area including Amazon-type review stars. All this comes at no extra cost to the advertiser but also comes with at least ten times the number of clicks.

SERPs are also giving more space to:

- Local area businesses together with addresses and phone numbers
- Images relevant to the search term

- Shopping sites relevant to the search term and using information shared by the advertiser in Google Merchant Center.

All this information is for advertisers, not for the free listings and with the focus on the top three advert spots on the left hand side of the SERP.

This shift towards advertisers in the SERPs is not surprising. 97% of Google's $59bn income comes from Google AdWords alone.

What is interesting is the 80/20 Google is performing for its advertisers who are being rewarded with the prize slots at no extra cost, more space for their adverts, more information in the adverts and the certainty of better click through rates.

Keep your eye on our website and its blog to keep up-to-date on the constant amendments and improvements to Google searches and how it affects you as an advertiser.

Chapter 9: **Develop (not trip over) your Unique Selling Point** – Unique Selling Propositions (USPs)

Everyone knows about USPs don't they? Or do they?

Every rookie marketer thinks he knows about USPs and can probably quote word for word from the marketing bible why you are supposed to create one.

But we want to get past the modern apologies for a USP and the unthinking following of decades of dead marketing advice that was probably already starting to age when it was first printed.

I haven't done the research on the life and times of USPs and I don't plan to. But I wonder if there was a time when businesses just thought it was luck to create a USP that was rare and memorable enough to turn a small town business into a global franchise.

Will the world see the likes of these again?:

> Domino's Pizza: 'You get fresh, hot pizza delivered to your door in 30 minutes or less—or it's free.'

FedEx: 'When your package absolutely positively has to get there overnight.'

If you examine these two USPs for a moment it's obvious that the guys who came up with the concepts were intent on establishing a lead for their enterprises. The phenomena tackled were aspirations of pizza shops and couriers respectively and are levels of service we take for granted today but unheard-of then. What they have in common is that no business person in their right mind would stick their necks out and commit themselves in such ways. But the rare ones developed ways to achieve the seemingly impossible and reaped the rewards.

The point is that to find a selling proposition that is unique enough to propel a small-town business to international franchise may be rare and so impossible that we are talking absolutes. Either the USP is so earth shattering and different (extremely rare) – or it isn't.

But there is a middle ground. Just because the USP might not be ending Amazon's strangle-hold of online sales (yet!) it is still possible to be different and unusual enough to be a serious threat to your competition.

'Best in the north-west' isn't going to hack it on any scale but 'same day delivery' could be seen as improbable enough by current standards to give a business a real advantage across the UK.

So now it's time to see if we can develop and create a shiny, new USP (and, of course, you can have as many USPs as you care to expand – if you are willing to put in the time and the effort (and ignore the strict meaning of 'unique').)

Develop is the operative word here. If your USP comes to you out of the blue – exploit your good fortune for all it is worth. Really good USPs take time and testing to get a right fit for your company and ruffle the feathers of the competition. Even better is a USP that soars above your rivals and leaves them on the ground in terms of value to the customer.

The good news is that development of USPs is possible. It is a process using several techniques and some concentrated work but the value is immeasurable. It's not magic and you don't need a rare talent. But you do need the will to stick at a task and see it through to completion.

Using these techniques a small businessman in the USA developed a USP and leapt way ahead of the competition. His selling proposition is still unique and has made him a lot of money, money that continues to pour in.

The business was in the niche market of delivery firms who drive cars across many miles of the country for its clients who presumably follow by plane. (This niche is small to vanishing in the UK because here we don't need to cover the distances they do in the States.) One of the hazards of the business is damage to the cars. Until our businessman came along it was just accepted by the clients who signed contracts exempting liability for those providing the service, that some of the cars would get damaged in transit.

Our hero devised a method so that he could guarantee cars wouldn't be scratched or in need of repair, the guarantee being that he would foot the repair bill. His competitors waited for him to go bust, but they're still waiting and his business is thriving.

This USP sounds falling-off-a-log easy to implement. It wasn't. The distance-delivery niche relies on come-day-go-day, sub-contract, self-employed drivers who bring no loyalty to their work. They complete a delivery half-way across the country, couldn't care less about the odd scratch to the paintwork, then drop the car off and look for another contract. Insuring them against bigger accidents is difficult and against dents and scratches impossible. Our hero didn't stumble across his crock of gold, he developed it with a lot of hard work, using lateral thinking and 80/20 (Chapter 7) to maximise his ideas for his new USP.

Of all the AfterBurners we offer, creation of USPs has the potential of lifting you into the stratosphere.

For more information on how to generate profit expanding USPs visit:

www.plannedsites.com/USPDevelopment

Chapter 10: **Getting it Right** – Elevator Pitch

It's early evening and you're in the bar of the hotel you're staying in on a business trip. There's just you and Bill, the barman, idly chatting when another man in a business suit comes in looking decidedly disgruntled with life.

'Largest scotch you've got, please Bill' he says.

'Everything not go according to plan then, sir?'

'Couldn't have been worse, Bill. My presentation fell flat on its face. I was relying on that sale and now I don't what we're going to do.'

'I was just speaking to this gentlemen' says Bill indicating you 'and it appears he may have an idea or two that could help you.Perhaps he has some suggestions.'

So, there you have it – Presentation of the Perfect Prospect.

But can you handle it? After a few minutes will you and Prospect-on-a-Plate end up shaking hands and exchanging business cards or will Prospect-on-a-Plate start getting bored with your stammering, uncoordinated ramble and start wondering if he can sidle out to dinner without seeming too rude?

This is where your Elevator Pitch comes in.

An Elevator Pitch is a comprehensive but succinct explanation of what your business does. It should be instantly understandable so that prospects can appreciate your value to them in the time it takes an elevator to travel from the 9th floor to the ground floor. It should definitely include your USP.

The existence of an Elevator Pitch makes all in the company who have committed it to memory instant salespersons.

The Elevator Pitch should also be pinned to the notice board of the marketing department and in the offices of the advertising agency. From the mail boy to the CEO – everyone should memorise your Elevator Pitch. It also acts as a great stimulus to creative minds for all publicity and advertising material including Google AdWords.

It should also be printed on the back of all business cards and reproduced on the website.

Another advantage of having a great Elevator Pitch is re-focusing attention on the most important aspects of the business. We've all been to meetings where two hours is lost to discussing a font face on a logo or colleagues disagree on what the marketing budget should be spent on. The Pitch allows everyone to take stock of what is really important to your business and progress in the same direction.

Constantly using it in these ways also keeps your pitch evolving. If a conscious decision is made by the company to shift its strategy it will need to rejuvenate its Elevator Pitch. This makes the strategy-shift a conscious decision, and not one drifted into over time. Following an ill-thought out or fragmented Elevator Pitch (one where members of the company are following different pitches) can be damaging to the business. Having consciously to update the Elevator Pitch means it is rolled out to everyone at the same time, and every employee should be aware of the new company focus and pitch.

Don't confuse Elevator Pitches with mottos or mission statements. Google famously uses 'Don't be evil' as a badge of honour. It would never be mistaken for an Elevator Pitch.

Chapter 11: **They Pay the Bills including Your Salary** – Dealing with your most valuable asset

What actually is your most valuable asset? Don't bother thinking about it for too long. Well in front of the rest of the field is your list of customers or clients, whatever you decide to call them – the guys who pay your bills. Let's give them a collective name – your list.

I've just been dealing with a client who retired and recently closed his business. Rather than just abandon his list he gave it away to a competitor – for FREE. He literally didn't realise it was worth money. I calculated he could have sold it for £650,000.

But a successful business owner who realises value when he sees it will tell you his list are what gives him greater security than his bank account. You could lose all your money today, and provided you have looked after and tended to your list, you would recoup those losses from your list *tomorrow.*

The thing about lists is that you don't want to end up with a diseased list, an inferior list, or a low-value list that is filled with 'cheap' customers who make your life miserable and constantly haggle with you on price and terms.

You want an exceptional list that you love doing business with – one that is loyal to you, and doesn't want to buy from anyone else.

Not only is it much more enjoyable to do business with a special list, but a special list means value. It means responsiveness. It means fairness.

There are a few important considerations when developing your special list.

First, you lose value in your list if you don't do things to sustain it. You have to follow-up and keep tending to the list. It doesn't take much time before they stray and join another estate owner – happy that you let them go for free, without dispute or complaint. Why go to all the trouble of collecting such a valuable stock – if you let them wander off aimlessly to benefit another business?

The thing about follow-ups in general is:

Most business people fail at it miserably.

If you discipline yourself and organise your business to capture full prospect and customer contact information, and then diligently invest in persistent follow-ups, you'll gain enormous competitive advantage.

Second, many business owners put too much emphasis on value and not enough emphasis on all the things that cause people to stay on a list.

Logic says if I give them value and I give them a lot of value for their money and they take what I sell them for 'X' and they use that to make 'Y' and as long as that happens again and again and again why would they ever leave me? Why would they stop coming back?

That's a logical, sensible return on investment approach to a relationship between a consultant, a coach, trainer, advisor, a publisher, etc. and a customer or a client, but it is fatally flawed. *Fatally flawed.*

That's not why people stay on a list. We can argue it should be why they stay on a list. But the truth is there is only a small percentage of people who stay for that reason.

People stay on a list because they feel a sense of belonging and pride of attachment. They stay because they feel you care about them and the results they get. They stay because they attach themselves to a belief system—a higher and more meaningful purpose that you share with them.

Why do people camp out at 4am in the morning, on a wet Monday in Solihull to buy the latest Apple product? It isn't because other products can't offer the same specifications (they do, and often for less money) it's because they completely and utterly identify with the ethos and identity that Apple projects. To the point of shunning all other business rivals and paying more cash in the process - for the privilege of being an Apple consumer. Entering an Apple shop is almost like a quasi-religious experience, where iPads and laptops are exalted to mythical status and reverence. Who wouldn't put effort into keeping this devout list loyal for life?

There are, of course, other factors too, such as frequency, consistency, and presence.

Frequency matters a lot.

Linked to frequency is consistency.

Consistency is institutionalised, standardised things happening, at the same time, at the same place, which meets a level of expectation ... anticipation. When you subscribe to a magazine, you expect it to come the second week of every single month like clockwork.

Presence. Do you have a presence in their everyday lives? In other words, if they look around, is there something in their everyday environment that is relevant to you? For example, go to a real football fan's house you will see evidence of his team; a flag decorated with his team's badge, a coffee mug in the kitchen, an autographed football on display ...

Recognise your list for what it is: the most valuable asset you have. And once you start promising valuable relationships with prospects and customers or clients, be sure to follow up to develop, sustain and surpass their expectations of what a business is capable of.

Chapter 12: **Reduce Stress Everywhere** – Fire a few customers

The bottom tier of your customer list (80/20 rule – Chapter 7) are the 14% who buy solely on price. They are also the ones who give you most grief (80/20 again) and take up most of the time taken by customers (more 80/20) and your time is precious.

So sell them to your competitors. That way you achieve several things:

1. You get rid of negative customers who are always whingeing
2. You get rid of those who find it difficult to continue living without 'doing a deal'
3. You get rid of tyre kickers
4. You get rid of the stress of dealing with all the baggage those three bring to your life
5. You have more time for more successful marketing.
6. The competitor you sell them to gets less time to compete with you
7. You have more cash in the bank
8. You save cash from the time saved on having to deal with these customers
9. You also have the comfortable feeling that once fired a customer isn't going to come back any time soon.

If 'selling customers' is an odd concept to you, do a Google search on either 'selling customer lists' or 'Business Brokers'.

Firing customers like this has the added advantage that you don't have to ring them and tell them – the first they know anything about it is when they get the letter (drafted by your Broker) telling them of the arrangement and that, under the terms of the agreement with your buyers, you aren't allowed even to talk to them.

Chapter 13: **The Baby and Bathwater** – The phone in internet marketing

The phone is the most mis-used and misunderstood tool at your disposal. Some don't even consider it of any value.

Let's go back fifteen years to 1999, when the so-called dot-com boom and bust was in full swing (and, incidentally, when Google was no more than a twinkle in its founders' eyes).

There may be one or two of my readers who were not about for the dot-com phenomenon or have forgotten what it was. The world (as in planet – the boom was not just confined to the UK) went mad. Companies were often created just to take advantage of the new website craze. They were backed by entrepreneurs and banks and, almost unbelievably for companies without any trading history, sometimes by the stock market.

HTML (then in version 1, now in version 5), the language of the World Wide Web as the new branch of the internet was called, was crude and manual connections over phone lines had to be made as broadband wasn't yet available. (Your modem dialled your ISP and you got charged for the phone call by the minute.)

It was assumed you just had to set up a website and sit back. The world would beat a path to your door, tripping over each other in their eagerness to put their hard-earned money in your hand. All you had to do was decide which product to sell and how it was going to make you your fortune.

It didn't work out like that. For obvious reasons. Some of the less obvious reasons are still being perpetuated today by many businesses. One is the attitude to using the phone.

The general view was that the phone was no longer needed for its original purpose, conversations. The website would be all that was needed. So much so that businesses began to regard the phone as obsolete. Lots of the new sites didn't have phone numbers listed ANYWHERE. Look for it as you may, you couldn't find it. In a lot of cases the number was ex-directory. The most important people in the universe – customers – had suddenly become non-people; they didn't appear to matter anymore. Only someone with godlike knowingness could tell us what the sales and marketing people were thinking of.

Anyway, that's where and when the anti-phone sentiment started. Many sites continue with it today which is even stranger. You would have thought that a fairly new website today would've shaken off the sins of the fathers by now and be back to embracing communication with its customers as a number one priority.

So, let's set out a phone strategy for the 21st century.

- Book yourself a decent BT landline number. None of this 0845 rubbish. Nor its spin-offs. I defy anyone outside Oftel to know what all the permutations are; the average customer would not have a clue. So anything that doesn't look like a proper landline number (01234 xxxxxx) is unacceptable. Even if you think that most people know that 0800 numbers are free, they're not free from mobiles. A further point is that a lot of home phone deals these days include free national calls to a BT landline.

- Show the number prominently on the right-hand side of the banner on your site and make sure the banner, complete with phone number, appears on every page of your site. If you think the number is about the right size, it's too small. If it gets in the way of the rest of your banner design, re-design the banner. Top right is now the conventional website place for phone numbers.

- Don't decorate the blasted thing. It's obvious it's a phone number so it doesn't need stock images of phones or coily bits of wire or, even worse, the word 'TEL' near it. It need lots of space round it so it can breathe properly and communicate clearly your phone number.

- Don't add an email address just to be helpful. Believe it or not, you're trying to encourage people to use the phone so don't give them an alternative.

- You're probably getting the impression I think you ought to be encouraging people to ring, so it least I got that bit right.

- Now, hold on to your hats because this is where this chapter starts to get interesting. Ready?

- Have a human being answer it.

- There, I've said it. Shall I repeat it, so there's no possibility of ambiguity? Here you go: employ a human being to answer it. Whoever answers should have enough knowledge to answer intelligently and politely. He or she should have a computer so that he or she can deal with queries quickly on, say, lost parcels and a check-list* for prospect/customer information.

- 'Whoa!' I hear you cry. 'What's all this going to cost?' Don't worry; it's quite manageable, when you work out the real benefits. And the competitive advantage is enormous. If you assume you pay your telephonist an annual salary of £25,000 and you consider associated overheads of the employment is also £25,000 pa, those give an annual cost of £50,000 to employ your telephonist. If a conversation is going to last five minutes, then the total cost to your company will be £2.29 per call. The detail of this calculation is on the website [www.plannedsites/CostPerCall] If you don't think £2.29 is a reasonable investment for five minutes with a prospect or customer, see Chapter 11 – 'Most Valuable Asset' and Chapter 14 – 'The Value of a Customer'

We're living in a supposed modern age – and there's nothing more modern than hearing: 'Press 1 for Sales, Press 2 for Refunds and Press 3 if you want to go to the loo', is there? Automated phone answering seems automatically to be installed as a virility emblem nowadays. A prospect or a customer, the most precious asset you have, wants to speak to you and you do your best to put him through to three different departments, before finally cutting him off. By the time he does (if ever) phone back you can be sure it'll be the Complaints Department he's asking for.

On the web there are several sites that list the ten greatest pleasures in life. From the lists presented may I pick a few:

1. Sex
2. A cold bottle of New Zealand Sauvignon Blanc Premier Cru
3. A book or play (anything actually) by Alan Bennett
4. Doing whatever people say you cannot do
5. Cricket in the sunshine at Lord's
6. Cruising on a motor yacht (ditto the sunshine) along the South Cornwall coast
7. Observing the first swallow of Spring

8. Dover sole
9. Lobster thermidor

And other luxuriant past-times but I personally would like one I haven't seen anywhere else –yet:

10. A real human being, answering a phone who can actually answer your questions without having to listen to 7 minutes of The Four Seasons being butchered on a speaker phone, as you're put on hold for the nth time that day.

Investing in a real person – who is consumer savvy (good customer relationship skills are an art) and intelligent will pay you dividends in customer loyalty, not to mention the extra products sold and profit made for the lifetime of your company.

* The check-list your telelphonist should have enables him or her to engage the caller in friendly conversation and elicit personal information about the caller for storing on the database for future use. For more information about how this is exploited go to

www.plannedsites.com/CustomerDetails.

(If you're at all puzzled by this ask yourself if an important customer whose wife receives a bunch of flowers on her birthday every year is ever likely to desert to the competition.)

Chapter 14: **A Calculation Guaranteed to Amaze** – Value of a customer

Few business people calculate the value of a customer, most often because it doesn't occur to them to do so or even that it's possible. But a moment's thought will tell them what a valuable figure it would be. Instead of guessing how much to spend on acquiring a customer they could make informed decisions based on accurate facts. Most often they'd realise they'd been turning down perfectly good opportunities as too expensive when they were actually laughably cheap.

Say the business is selling children's clothing for an average of £8.00 per item and customers bought 1.5 items on average.

Average sales value is £8.00 x 1.5 = £12.00

At this point you should take off the VAT included in the sale because you have to hand that over to the government but here we're selling children's clothing which is zero-rated for VAT – so the sales value of the average transaction remains at £12.00*.

The policy of the business is to maintain a profit on its sales of 50% – in other words it doubles its cost price to arrive at its sales price. (This is just a rough guide used for this example – the actual profit target would change depending on product and the market your business was in.) The item costing £6 is therefore sold for £12 giving the target profit of £6.

Many businesses would say that £6 is therefore the value of that customer. This is a naïve and short-sighted mistake to make. The actual value of that customer is £630 as I will explain. (That's correct: 105 times the number most people would first think of.)

Let's pick up the argument again at the inaccurate presumption that our customer example is only worth £6 and take it a few steps further.

Your quality, your standards of service and the overall positive feeling your website creates, causes your average new customer to order clothes for her children six times a year plus Christmas – this equals seven times a year. If she tells an average of five of her friends and relations about your site they become customers as well – some of them ordering an average amount. A few (remembering the 80/20 law (chapter 7)) will order a lot more.

First the supposed value of this new customer can be increased by seven-fold, the number of sales in a year. That is the profit of £6 on the average first sale times the number of sales (seven) and equals £42.

Second the customer has told five of her pals. We can therefore multiply the new value calculated in the previous paragraph by five giving a value of £42 x 5 equals £210.

There is a further factor. Business brokers ratchet up the annual value of a customer by the number of years the customer is expected to remain a customer. You could argue that our business, if it's doing its job properly, could expect to retain an average customer for an average of ten years. But life's not like that, so the broker would adjust the factor down to match real life. We'll be ruthless about it and mark it down from ten years to three. So that new customer is now being valued at £210 times three equals £630.

The value of a customer is therefore £630 or 105 times the value the business first thought.

As I said at the beginning of this chapter, many businesses will turn down the opportunity to make money as the perceived cost of the click seems at the outset too high.

For example, say a click costs £7. Say also your conversion rate it 20%, meaning you are converting one in five click-throughs to customer status. That means the total cost of a conversion is £7 times 5 which equals £35. Some people would be put off by that cost. But not those who have calculated that the value of a customer is £630 (or whatever your calculation came to when working out the value of your customer). They will be more than happy to pay out £35 to acquire a customer worth £630.

While we're on the subject, beware being lulled into thinking that a 50p click-through (achieved by erroneously using inappropriate keywords because they are 'cheap') is bound to be better value than a £5 click-through. It's only better value when the arithmetic in the previous paragraph says so. The price of a keyword is determined by auction, not by the whim of a Google employee; the price is therefore likely to reflect true value.

The Americans call the false logic of using click-through costs only (that is without conversion stats) 'leaving money on the table' to which I would only add 'for their competitors to collect'.

We've put a spreadsheet on our website to do this calculation for you. Go to

www.plannedsites.com.com/ValueOfCustomer.

Before estimating the cost of any advertising campaign, especially Google AdWords – remember to work out the true value of that new customer that you maybe wavering over. The real cost is the actual survival and future prosperity of your business.

*Many businesses not registered for VAT could do so and receive VAT refunds on VAT they've paid on their bills. It's not for everyone but a business selling exclusively children's clothing should seriously consider it. For more go to

www.plannedsites.com/ShouldIRegisterForVAT.

Chapter 15: **Getting All that is Due to You** – Premium Pricing

Have a look round your neighbourhood next time you're out with a view to satisfying yourself what you and everyone accepts – that people buy on price. You soon realise that everything is not what as it seems:

- On the roads, in the driveways and filling the car parks are cars which are often this year's model – even though a car depreciates in value as much as 30% the first day you take it off the garage forecourt. Repeatedly the most expensive makes and models are outselling the more economical choices and the luxury version often outstrips the demand for the more basic (and cheaper) version

- There a wide variety of restaurants in the high street and the numbers in each seem to fly in the face of the prices on the menus.

- And so is the fact that *anyone* is eating in the restaurants at all. If people bought on price restaurants would go out of business. You pay four times the supermarket price for the food

- First deliveries of Jersey Royal potatoes sell for £6.20 a kilogram, ordinary potatoes ('scrubbers', we used to call them) for less than £1

- Starbucks sell a coffee for around £3.50 when you could buy a whole jar of it for that. They don't even mention a price on their website. But they do let you know about the quality of their Colombia Nariño roasted coffee beans, their Mobile Wi-Fi Community and their Coffee Tastings. This is not a place to just drink coffee, it's an immersive new culture and way of life they want you to buy into. If you're willing to pay for the privilege – and 10.5 million cups are sold every day worldwide – plenty of people do and will

If you do a spot of research, you'll find only 14% of people buy on price. The other 86% account for the list above. We like to think we're rational, logical, beings but most of our decisions are based on feeling and emotion. It's the reason why in taste tests, customers repeatedly say Pepsi tastes better – but consistently buy Coca Cola instead.

Further afield, consider these:

- The most sought-after mobile phone in the world is the most expensive
- Seats on one of the most uncomfortable planes in recent times – the Concorde – were in the first-class plus price category. And the planes were always full
- The more expensive the car, the longer the waiting list

The implications for marketers who understand these phenomena are profound (and profit accumulating). Internet marketing is enhanced greatly as well as traditional marketing, but with the additional advantages that effective price changes can be implemented quickly and testing can be done easily and feedback received quickly.

Pricing strategy is vital or it's an ill-considered guess – and getting it wrong can mean a cut in profits.

The upside of getting your pricing strategy right?

- Increased returns
- Putting your time into making quality products and services – instead of watching like a hawk the incremental price changes of all your competitors
- Selling to customers who are prepared to buy on price and quality (not tyre-kickers who waste time, and if in a blue moon they do actually part with their cash, will bargain you down to the lowest price they possibly can)
- Savings in time, effort and stress from avoiding these chancers

Most businesses don't know how to price properly for maximum benefit. Nearly all pricing is too low, driven by a fear of losing existing customers – or getting no customers at all in the case of start-ups.

It needs a deeper understanding of customer decision-making processes.

The first mistake is to charge what everyone else is. Put yourself back in the driving seat and control the price that your service or product is *actually* worth. Not what you think people are prepared to pay.

There are two main price issues:

1. Price pressure. Customers complain and look for deals. Present culture dictates that prices should be low, especially as they can now look easily on comparison sites and hunt for 'bargains'. It's not the customers' issue that they want a good deal – but it is your issue (if you wish to make a healthy profit) that you educate her about the worth of your product or service. If you can't do this – then don't expect

the customer to give you a bonus payment or pay a true price of what your business provides in value to them

2. The economy. Culture has changed in the latest recession and people don't spend like they used to. We feel we have to cut prices to stay competitive. It's fatal. The long-term consequences are:

    a. Cutting prices makes you like a commodity, akin to a shovel. People definitely buy shovels on price. You don't want to be a shovel

    b. Once you're a commodity you'll get hammered on price. If they see you as interchangeable with your competitors, then they'll just go with the cheapest. Differentiate clearly why they get value for shopping with you. (You can even do this selling the same products as your competitors – but changes in branding, buying experience and service quality all will make a difference to what your customers are willing to pay.)

    c. Low cost pricing sends the wrong messages to customers. If something's as 'cheap as chips' we're inclined to think the service or product will be as well

    d. It sets low expectations. Once prices are cut, customers may get into the habit of waiting for next price cut

Be more than just a peddler.

Cultivate your customers. Position yourself so you can develop them, and how they feel about you, regard you and interact with you. They need educating on why you are worth the higher prices (and make sure you are worth it!) and be clear on the benefits to them and the impact on their lives of such a product or service.

The better the value and marketing, the higher the prices you can command. If your marketing marks you out from the competition and communicates the benefits of shopping with you (even for commodities) you're likely to be able to charge a higher price than your competitor.

Price rise?

Panic!

Feel the fear but do it anyway:

1. Simply raise the price
2. Change the proposition:
   a. If the first thing every customer buys is £50, change it to £80. It won't feel like a price increase to your first-time customer, but it is.
   b. Increase the core product. Instead of, say, a massage, change it to a massage and a facial. Then double the price. It's often easier to get a fair price for lower priced items that attract unfair questioning of value, by bundling products or services.
   c. Be prepared to test it.
3. Introduce a deluxe or premium version. Interflora used to sell roses for £20. They still do, but now they offer a £350 hand-tied version as well. This is at no risk as they produce them on order only. It also boosts sales at the lower level as the premium products make the standard products look more reasonable in price
4. Introduce a payment plan. 6 x £195 seems a lot cheaper than £975 but it is actually a price increase of 20%

5. Add-ons can be bought very cheaply. Is there a basic product or service to which you can add extras that would increase value to your customer and increase your profits?
6. Discounts for the wealthy. The affluent love a deal. Buy two, get one free sounds much better than 33% discount

High-end customers don't like having to wait, so creating a waiting list just increases the desire to have the product.

Level one of premium pricing is to treat all customers the same. They all pay the same opening price, they all face the same price increase. Taking it to the next level recognises not all customers are the same. A proportion will always buy the premium version (80/20 – Chapter 7), if the perceived value is worth it.

Good marketing

Your customer will pay the price you ask if he feels the value you offer merits the payment. Good, effective marketing means getting the customer to appreciate the value of what you offer.

With services a lot of people have hang-ups about charging what they're really worth.
Think about what you've gone through to get where you are:

- Risks including any financial debt you've taken on
- Ups and downs, and putting your heart and soul into creating products and services.
- The hidden costs of running your business that the customer never sees or even wants to think about
- Inflation rises
- Working unsociable hours or even working bank holidays or weekends without extra payment

- Meeting a shorter deadline than expected (that the customer suddenly sprung on you) which you duly accommodate. With no thought for the juggling of your other customers or time you've had to conjure from somewhere else
- The value that product or service provides in the long run. Charging by the hour may be the way all your competitors do business, but if you could show the value of what a customer gained from your service over the long term – isn't that a fairer price for your skills than being paid like the local shelf stacker in Tescos? And if you do happen to be a shelf stacker in Tescos, and you are the fastest and most reliable in the land – that too has a value to someone, somewhere. Think of the long term benefit of everyone you serve and tell them about it. Red Adair once said 'If you think it's expensive to hire a professional to do the job, wait until you hire an amateur.'

How much do you think you're worth?

For all products and services you are the worst person to decide what to charge. So test it and let the market decide.

1. If you have a new customer- just increase the price by 10% and see what happens.
2. Segment your product list and or your customer list or both, apply an increase on a segment and see what happens. For example customers who are under 25, or customers who live in a certain postcode.

Use anchor points to your advantage

Research has shown that the savviest of us can be swayed by suggestion even if we know the suggestion has no connection with the question we are addressing.

If a roulette wheel lands on three and we are then asked to guess a value of something we had no hope of valuing, then our guess will be within reaching distance of three. The same applies if the roulette wheel had produced 16; our guess will be within reaching distance of 16.

Don't believe the brain would fall for such a trick? Try asking someone the time and, right after, asking how many countries there are in Africa. The answer they supply (given that they are not the editor for the National Geographic) will be alarmingly close to the minute hand of their watch.

Psychologists call the roulette wheel values 'anchor points' and price consultants are now using this branch of psychology for increased revenue and sales.

Chapter 16: **Follow your Visitors after They Leave your Site:** Remarketing – a powerful trick but hardly used by SMEs

This is where we introduce you to a sleeping-giant of marketing techniques. Remarketing.

Never heard of it before? You're not alone – this internet marketing technique is chronically under-used (and when it is used is often not used to its full potential), misnamed, and often misunderstood – even by the marketing 'experts' themselves, who will try to convince you they make the most of this untapped potential for you.

So what is it?
You've gone to a shoe shop online, checked out the latest styles, and even browsed a few products that you could be interested in at a later point, but for now – you're just happy to check out the prices. Clicking off the site, you go back to browsing the internet only to see the shoes on the very site you were viewing an hour before, pop up on a totally un-related website. They're 'remarketing' to you.

This is just the beginning of what remarketing can do for your business…

For starters, all the internet marketing practitioners will tell you that remarketing applies to those who have visited your site. In fact the very term 'remarketing' implies that, doesn't it? Let me have the pleasure of being the first to tell you that your audience has a much bigger potential than that, by using Google's Display advertising 'Targeting' feature. This means that you can target a segment of visitors who have never been on your site and display your adverts on a related site or subject that is linked to your product or service. For example, a segment of potential customers who viewed racing bicycle wheels on your website, could now be shown those specific products on an advert displayed on a racing bike blog at a later date.

Almost without exception the marketing specialists will tell you that the 'classic' example of the use of remarketing is in getting back shoppers who abandoned the shopping cart process on your website. This shopping-cart example has become a 'classic' because it's so over-used. You can, of course, use a remarketing advert to remind her of her once-intended purchase with perhaps an incentive (discount, free delivery, voucher for future purchases or whatever you think would most entice this shopper to buy) to return and complete her purchase.

But an abandoned shopping cart isn't the most positive of examples to demonstrate the range and breadth of what this fantastic marketing tool can do.

Remarketing gives you the opportunity of speaking to someone who has visited your site and may or may not have bought something. You can talk to her about related products, new products to your range, seasonal sales, bundled offers . . . the list is endless. You can repeat the advert and update the advert. With care (there is a danger of overdoing it) you can talk to her for several months. You can also stop repeating adverts of any items the visitor subsequently buys off you.

Here're a few examples of what you can do with re-marketing:

- Offer products that need to be replaced at various intervals such as an oil change - this approach can be enhanced with advanced techniques, such as time sensitive displaying of adverts.
- Offer a different product or offer after a suitable interval of time and then another product after a further interval, say six over a six-month period. You'd restrict the number of times the advert was shown to avoid being a nuisance but you'd increase exponentially the chances of gaining a customer. (While researching Chapter 13 I visited some Cornish fishing sites looking for lobster. One of them started following me around (and still is) but only with pictures of fish. He didn't exploit the situation completely, missing out on the opportunity to convert me to a customer worth at least £630 (see Chapter 14) with a few clicks and some out-of-the-box thinking. If that fishrmonger is reading this (and I'm going to send him a copy of the book – so he should) please look at www.plannedsites.com/CornishFV For my other readers – if you also visit that page you'll see a detailed example of this brilliant concept in action, and if you use this technique itself, you will gain a steady stream of great value customers).
- You can build a landing page for an individual, using her buying habits (in other words her conversions on your site) and your product lines stored in the Google Merchant Center.
- Use remarketing to announce a seasonal sale
- Include remarketing in all product launches
- Use remarketing to make time-limited offers of bundled products only to remarketed visitors – 'buy

x and y for special price of £z; offer ends on Thursday midnight'

- Offer a discount or free shipping (but hopefully you're now offering free shipping as part of your basic service anyway) as an extra incentive
- Offer an upsell or cross-sell
- Offer a free gift
- Show a recent review or testimonial about your particular product or service
- Repeat your USP
- Show more detail of product originally viewed
- Use your thank-you page to its maximum potential and ask your customer to sign up to a newsletter. You already have got them to buy from you, so it would only take a small push in buyer commitment to get them to sign-up, especially if you offer them must-have savings or latest product launches they get to see first
- If the original page the customer viewed was a landing page and they then left it, you know they didn't think much of what was on the landing page – but you do know what search terms they used to get there, where they are in the sales funnel and what type of product or service they are interested in. They may even have clicked through from a printed advert or an email. You now have a great second chance of making an even better landing page to capitalise on the interest you know they have. Very few advertising media (if any) give you such great opportunity to improve upon your first attempt and win that sale back

As I remarked earlier you can use the targeting feature of the Google AdWords Display network to widen your audience by up to millions. Your audience is then those who have specifically visited your webpages plus those of a target category on the new websites your adverts are displaying on. However, this should only be used if the advert is not too focused on previous visitors and could be shown to a much wider audience running into millions, and would have a cross-over interest where the adverts are to be displayed.

The difficult part of using this exciting system whose potential we have only touched on is remembering the advert has to be aimed at segment of shopper and not at an individual.

Learn more about the explosive potential of remarketing for your business, here:

www.plannedsites.com/Remarketing

Chapter 17: **Get into Google's Good Books** – Google Merchant Center

Ever wondered where all those product images come from on a modern Google results page? Google Merchant Center (GMC), that's where. GMC is a data feed that you upload to Google (as often as you like to keep it up-to-date) with details of all your products. The GMC is also the source for

1. Google's Shopping results page. (You'll see the Shopping page link at the top of a Google results' page.)
2. Dynamic Remarketing. Remarketing is an underused, misunderstood tool in the internet marketing toolbox (more in Chapter 16) and we advocate implementation at the earliest opportunity. Dynamic remarketing, introduced by Google only a year ago, takes remarketing and links it to your entry in GMC to provide a variety of alternatives from your range to your visitors who have clicked off product pages previously.

Google is very fussy about the quality of the data feed. It has to be in a prescribed format which is based on a spreadsheet. Most businesses run accounting software these days that have an export function from your product database. This can usually be adapted to act as the GMC data feed.

Chapter 18: **The Ultimate Accolade**
Write the book

Many of us could write a book.

Many of us are encouraged to write a book. You may have been told by colleagues 'you should write a book.' Often it's after we've served 50 years in the same job and we're picking up the jubilee clock to commemorate the time spent dedicated to someone else's endeavour.

Many of us fancy writing a book.

Few of us do.

Those who do 'get round to it' are then put off by the hurdles:

- Planning the structure
- Writing the damn thing
- Spelling isn't the horror it once was by the provision of spell-checkers on word processors but what about grammar? And, to some, punctuation is a nightmare.
- Finding a publisher, particularly if the subject is in a narrow niche market
- The apprehensions about achieving a minimum sale

Those not put off by the hurdles look forward to many business advantages which, of course, is why there is this chapter devoted to the subject in this book:

- The title of this chapter is 'Write *the* book' not 'Write *a* book', as in 'He wrote the book'. I have written this book because I am the inventor of a new approach to internet marketing, an approach that is also our USP. Now, claiming to be the inventor of something is good and picks up Brownie points. But, for some reason, nothing brings in the accolades and reverence of being able to say 'I wrote the book'.
- Having the book on sale on Amazon boosts the reputation as well. Anyone doubting your credentials can be referred by way of URL to the Amazon sales page.
- You become known as the go-to expert on your chosen book subject
- Signed copies of the book can be sold off the website's Home page
- Signed copies of the book can be given away as incentives on the website – which is maybe why you're reading this
- In summary, 'writing the book' allows you to claim authority in your field of endeavour like very little else with the possible exception of winning a Nobel prize.

Having obviously been through the exercise we can offer expert guidelines and assistance to making your book a success:

www.plannedsites.com/WriteTheBook

End Notes … but . . . see you soon

Internet marketing is a never-ending stream of learning and excitement so this book will be continually updated . . . FREE of charge.

We will be adding new chapters. As they are completed PDF copies will be emailed to all subscribers of the book FREE of charge. When the time is ripe (at the moment we're aiming for the second half of 2015) we will consolidate the new chapters into the book and a copy of the second edition will also be FREE to all subscribers of this first edition.

Please register for the FREE updates and a FREE copy of the second edition at www.plannedsites.com/Updates

At the time of publication of the book (Autumn 2014) these are the additional chapters that are planned or in production:

Laser Targeting your Prospect – the traditional marketing art of using personas brought sharply up-to-date with a modern technique.

Don't Leave the Easiest Money on the Table – the extraordinary habit of website owners of not saying 'thank you'

properly as their mummies taught them.

Straight Out of Left Field – Lateral thinking has a place in every business

Website Structure, Design and Content – Avoid the dreaded fate of losing prospects before they've bought, particularly the **over 50%** of shopping carts that are abandoned before checkout.

Customers Galore and in Double-Quick Time – A video that goes viral on YouTube may be a fluke but similar success with websites can be planned.

The New Yellow Pages – Google's laid siege to a venerated market with Google Local.

Suggestions for new chapters are not only welcomed but will be rewarded by a FREE copy of one of our instructional videos when the suggestion is adopted. Please go to

www.plannedsites.com/Suggestions

And don't forget to register for the FREE PDFs and a FREE copy of the second edition:

www.plannedsites.com/Updates

Index

Internet marketing – A New Approach